How to Make Passive Income with Affiliate Marketing

Set Up Your Business Once, Make Passive Income for Life!

Malcom Berry

Table of Contents

Chapter I
What is Affiliate Marketing

Online Affiliate Marketing is a revenue sharing venture between a website owner and an online merchant. The website owner will place advertisements on his websites to either help sell the merchant's products or to send potential customers to the merchant's website, all in exchange for a share of the profits.

Affiliate Marketing Program

An affiliate marketing program may be referred to as a pay-for-performance program or an associate program. An affiliate program is a marketing tool for the e-business that operates it, called merchant or advertiser and a source of revenue for the e-business that participates in it, called an affiliate or associate or publisher.

There are three ways to earn money through affiliate marketing:

1. Pay per Click or Cost-per-click affiliate programs:

Every time a potential customer leaves the affiliate website by "clicking" on the link leading to the merchant's website, a certain amount of money is deposited in the affiliate's account. This amount can be pennies or dollars depending on the product and amount of the commission.

2. Pay per Lead or Cost-per-lead affiliate programs

The merchant pays the affiliate a set fee for each visitor who clicks through and takes and action at the merchant's site, such as completing an online survey, registering at the site, or opting-in to receive e-mail.

3. Pay per Sale or Cost-per-sale affiliate programs

Every time a sale is made as a result of advertising on the affiliate's website, a percentage, or commission, is deposited into the affiliate's account.

The Amazon Story

The world's biggest bookstore has one of the most successful examples of an affiliate program (called their associate program). Amazon now has well over 1 million affiliates! That is over 1 million websites actively promoting their products every single second of every single day.

Amazon generates over 40% of its revenue through its affiliates program. That is over $3 billion in revenue every single year.

As another (somewhat humble by comparison) example, Zeald generates over 50% of its revenue using its own unique affiliates program. Admittedly, not quite billions of dollars but that is definitely millions of dollars of revenue every single year.

Thousands of diverse e-businesses operate affiliate programs: E.g. barnes & noble, dell,1-800-flowers, rackspace managed hosting etc.

Affiliate Programs as a Marketing Tool

The two major Advantages to merchant

1. Tie marketing effort directly to a lead or sales.

2. The merchant pays only for results.

The two major Advantages to affiliate

1. Additional source of revenue for affiliate who also sells products/services

2. Primary source of revenue for affiliate who offers entertainment or information

How to Be Successful with Affiliate Marketing

- Join a huge affiliate program like amazon

- RVPart - Sells parts for recreational vehicles and motor homes.

- Dilbert - Site for view cartoons, play games, send electronic greeting cards etc.

- HaperCollins - Its site to promote its authors and their books. However, like many book publishers. HaperCollins sells its books through bookstores and not directly to the public.

- Acquire a smaller number of highly effective affiliates that have a high volume of website traffic and offer web page content, products and services that are directly related to the merchant's products and services.

Affiliate Programs as a Revenue Source

Participating in an affiliate program and then getting the most out of your participation involves:

- Selecting the appropriate merchant and affiliate program for your e-business

- Understand the terms of the affiliate agreement

- Add custom links to merchant's site from affiliate Web pages

- Build traffic at affiliate site to increase click-thru rate to merchant site.

Top 10 Tips for Choosing the Affiliate Program That Is Right for You

1. You have to identify a product or service for which there is a need. The product should be something you love and enjoy promoting it. You could start by searching for "Affiliate Programs" in the Search Engines.

2. The product or service should be relevant to your website.

3. It is always wise to join an affiliate program that is long standing, safe and secure and has a good reputation in the Internet world. This can be easily verified from the Better Business Bureau or other similar organizations.

Visits to Forums and Discussion Groups will also provide you with lots of useful information.

4. Most affiliate program providers provide a commission of 5% to 50%. The commission you earn for the sale of a product is your main income.

So while choosing an affiliate program you should promote a product with commission pay out of 35% or more.

5. There should be a proper tracking system in place to record all the clicks and sales made through the text links and banners placed on your website, e-mails and other advertisements.

6. One important factor that is often overlooked is the "hits per sale ratio". This indicates the number of hits that have to be made to a Text Link or Banner to generate a sale. This will give you an idea as to how much traffic is needed before a sale is made.

7. How often are commissions paid? This is another important matter that should be considered. Most reputed organizations pay their affiliates monthly or when they accumulate a minimum commission of $50 to $ 100 or as indicated by you. You should avoid any program that requires too many sales to reach the minimum amount.

8. Affiliate Programs are generally single tier or two tiers. A single tier program pays you for whatever business you have generated.

On the other hand a two tier program pays you for the business you have generated and also a commission for the sales generated by a sub- affiliate, you have sponsored. A two tier program is always advantageous.

9. Long standing reputable organizations provide a whole range of tools and resources such as Banners, Text Links, Brochures, Websites and

training for their affiliates. When choosing a affiliate program, look out for such organizations because they certainly make life much easier and helps you grow your home based business.

10. Finally, you must read and understand the agreement before you join as an affiliate even if it happens to be the best organization in the world.

Affiliate management networks

An affiliate management network is a third-party entity that recruits affiliates, manages the registration process, tracks and properly credits all of the fee and commissions and arranges for payment.

In return for these services, the affiliate management network collects from the merchant a percentage of each referral transaction's fee or commission-perhaps as much 30 percent.

Well-established affiliate management networks: Example: Commission Junction, LinkShare

Affiliate tracking technologies

To achieve this we develop a strategic online relationship with advertisers to improve the creation, management, and analysis of online marketing and sales activities. These activities are supported by a scalable and reliable tracking technology.

Keeping track of the click-throughs and properly crediting the affiliates is a complex programming task.

Companies such as **BeFree** and **ClickTrade** sell software that automatically monitors and credits all followed links resulting in a sale.

Note that **ClickTrade** was acquired by Microsoft and is now co-branded as part of Microsoft bCentral.

Some tracking technologies are following:

- Custom links containing affiliate information or affiliate and merchant information

- Tracking cookies

- Third-party tracking software

- Application service provider tracking service

- Sub Domain tracking

- Database record matching

Affiliate Marketing Risks and Challenges

Affiliate marketing is not without certain risks and challenges, primarily form unethical affiliates and the negative perceptions online consumers have about tracking technologies.

Unethical Affiliates

- Cookie stuffing - Multiple cookies placed on visitor's hard drive during a single visitor affiliate site

- Spyware - General term used to describe software that has been installed on a personal computer without the owner's permission, its unknowingly download and install spyware when you download games, screensavers, freeware utilities and so forth.

- Parasiteware - Redirects affiliate links and Replaces content of existing tracking cookies

- Spammers - Merchant is responsible if affiliates use spam to promote sites

- Negative perception of tracking cookies - Many consumers install and use blocking software which includes Block tracking cookies and Delete tracking cookies.

Chapter II
Why Affiliate Marketing Is Profitable for E-Business

If you have been considering an affiliate marketing venture, there are some very good reasons why you should go with this method of generating recurring revenue.

Here are some of the ways that affiliate marketing can be a lucrative means of creating income that will be stable and allow you to grow exposure over time.

- One of the first advantages of affiliate marketing for the new entrepreneur is that the startup cost is very low. Most companies that offer affiliate marketing programs do not require any type of monetary investment on the part of the affiliate.

- The second expenses are limited to what you have to pay to connect with the Internet, the software you may need to load on your computer, and a web site where the ads associated with the affiliate marketing program can be placed.

Since web hosting is so inexpensive service these days, setting up your own web site for the affiliate ads will be a breeze.

- Another reason that affiliate marketing is such a moneymaker is the fact that there are so many different types of ways to set up the program.

You can go with the pay per click option, which works out great when it comes to promoting special offers.

Ads that lead to product review sites often are a way to allow product users to go through your portal and leave comments on the items they purchase.

First Thing's First.
Avoid These Silly Affiliate Marketing Mistakes!

While affiliate marketing is a great way to earn a living, the fact is that many people become discouraged and drop out of programs.

In many instances, the failure to be successful with affiliate marketing has to do with making a few simple mistakes. Here are some examples of those mistakes and why they should be avoided.

- A low-quality website with no original content and tossing in some affiliate links.

While it is certainly true that you need to have a web site up and running in order to participate in an affiliate program, there is also the need to apply some effort to getting the word out about your site.

Otherwise, the chances of people visiting your web site and clicking on one of the links are pretty slim.

- Another mistake many affiliate partners make is not choosing products that have some relevance to the content of your web site.

- Keeping your site content and the ads more or less relevant to one another will make it easier to generate revenue, and not fail as an affiliate marketer.

Now, this may seem intuitive - but many make this mistake in subtle ways (i.e. they mismatch their customers with products).

- One final mistake that many affiliate marketers make is not sprucing up their web sites from time to time.

Keeping the content fresh is one way of building and keeping a loyal reading audience because keeping the same old look and the same old text with nothing new to entice people back is a sure way to limit your chances at being a successful affiliate marketer.

The fact is that you do have to proactively promote your site, keep the content fresh, and make sure the ads have some connection to the subject matter of your site.

What You Need Before Getting Started and Affiliated Marketing

While there is not a lot of expense in starting up as an affiliate marketer, there are a few things that you need to do if you really want to make money marketing other people's products.

Here are some basic tips to help you line up all your things to do before you ever sign up for that first affiliate program.

- One of the basic needs for any successful affiliate program is to have a web site of your own. While it is possible to purchase ad space on sites and to advertise through Google Adwords, this is short term strategy setting up a basic web site that has a particular focus will make all the difference in the world to the success of your program. Keep in mind that your web site does not have to be complicated with a lot of flash media, animation or other fancy bells and whistles.

- In fact, if you plan on focusing your attention on affiliate marketing strategies that target the home consumer, you are better off with a basic site that will load quickly on a dial up connection. After all, dial-up is still extremely popular in a number of locations.

- Online payments are a great way to easily receive your affiliate payments and keep track of your earnings. From this angel, you may want to look into opening an account with one of the more popular online services that send and receive funds…PayPal.

- Another important aspect is determining just what your contact information will be, regarding communication with your affiliate program. This would include an email Address and physical mailing address. The email address should be one you have set aside specifically for your marketing business.

How to Pick the Best Product with the Best Payout and Great Demand

- One of the first things to think in terms of when it comes to affiliate marketing is determining where your talents and expertise happen to reside.

One of the keys to picking the best products for your particular situation have to do with what you know and how much you know about it.

As an example, a person that has worked in telecommunications for a number of years will probably know a great deal about telephon related services, and technology that are used within that industry.

- Another aspect about setting up with the right products to promote has to do with where you see a niche to fill in.

Finding a population or business sector that appears to be largely ignored in the marketing process can provide the inspiration you need to create a successful affiliate marketing program.

- Do not allow yourself to get discouraged simply because everything is not crystal clear as you begin this part of the process.

Practicing some patience and giving yourself time to find the right products to promote as part of the program will only serve to make you more dedicated to the success of the program.

In the end, you will find the products that will lead to a very successful affiliate marketing scheme and provide you with not only a handsome revenue stream, but also a lot of personal satisfaction.

Recommended Top Affiliate Networks on the Internet

When you decide to enter the world of affiliate marketing, there are a number of markets that are worthy of consideration.

Here are three programs that have captured the attention of a lot of people, simply because of their stability and reliability.

1. Perhaps the best known of the three programs is Clickbank. There are a number of reasons why people find ClickBank such an attractive option when it comes to affiliate programs.

One aspect is that the revenue generated by any purchase made through the ad portal is credited to your account within two minutes of the completion of the transaction. Clickbank provides such a comprehensive tracking program.

2. pavdotcom is also an excellent choice as an affiliate network. Just as with Clickbank, PayDotCom provides an easy to use affiliate interface that allows you to view your numbers in real time.

You can easily track such data as the number of clicks on the ads and the amount of commissions you have made by directing visitors over to the marketplace through the portal on your web site.

One of the advantages of PayDotCom is that this program will interface with your PayPal account, which means that vendors can send your monthly commission directly to your PayPal account.

It is important to note that not all vendors will use PayPal as a payment method, so you may still receive payments by check as well.

3. Shareasale is a third option that is rapidly gaining recognition among affiliate marketers. As a program that is designed to match up to the content of your existing web site, Shareasale is free to join as an affiliate.

Rising to the Super Affiliate Level

What Constitutes a Super Affiliate?

A super affiliate is a marketing affiliate that has created a network that provides a high volume of traffic to affiliate products and a high percentage of completed sales from that traffic. The super affiliate is not one who reaches this level once, or even once in a great while.

- Creativity is an hallmark of a super affiliate. The ability to present the same old information in new ways will keep people interested.

Super affiliates know how to look at products from a variety of different angles, determine a series of ways to present the product, and then go out and find an audience to match up with each one of those ways.

For the super affiliate, there is always one more way to draw attention to a product, and find a larger audience than ever before.

- Another characteristic of a super affiliate is the desire and ability to master technology.

This does not necessarily involve becoming an expert in information technology. But it does involve learning enough about existing technology to make good use of avenues already open on the Internet to promote products.

- Making the most of your status as a super affiliate means enjoying the opportunities that come to you through word of mouth; additionally, it means taking matters into your own hands and promoting your status in such a way that you increase your visibility.

The Super Affiliate Marketing Tactics Exposed!

So what is it that allows a super affiliate to make hundreds or even thousands of sales when you struggle to make 5 sales of the same product?

Why is that super affiliates rake in the cash while you struggle to get by? Think about this carefully: you are both selling the exact same product.

The only possible difference is the tactics you use to market it. Below, we have included a couple tactics that we should use to sell more like super affiliates. Try to incorporate them into your strategy.

Tactic #1: Play the Long Game

Whenever some new launch is coming up, they will throw together a promotional website; and try to direct traffic to it using pay per click search engine advertisements or solo ads.

But there is a major flaw with this approach: almost without exception, people will purchase a "big launch" product from an Internet marketer they already know.

This is why you have to play the long game, rather than focusing on each individual launch, prepare an approach that will work consistently for years to make more sales.

Tactic #2: Steal from Super Affiliates Whenever Possible

Many super affiliates are also big name Internet marketers. They have public personas that we can follow quite easily. We can find their user ld's, blogs, mailing lists and their web site's. Through this approach we can learn from each of them.

Tactic #3: Ignore Talk; Look for Revealed Preference

Talk is just that: talk. Many Internet marketers will talk about all sorts of different methods you can use to make money. They will tell you to advertise using Google AdWords or to build a list or to create viral reports.

While some of this information may be useful and legitimate, we should ignore what they say and watch what they do. This is called "revealed preference".

Tactic #4: Make Friends with the Seller

Believe it or not, the seller wants you to be successful, too. So contact him ahead of time, make friends with him; and see if he has any particular advice for you on selling the product. Keep in mind that he talks to a lot of affiliates on a regular basis (especially around big launches) and has the best understanding of the tactics they actually use.

Become a Supreme Affiliate Marketing: Additional Supreme Affiliate Marketing Tips

If you want to make a six figure income - and possibly a seven figure income - then you have to do something that is truly different than what you are doing now. The big question is "how can I do this"? Here are some suggestions:

Tip #1: Start Acting Like a Business Owner

If you want to be a successful affiliate product marketer, you have to find people who can augment your weakness (and, trust me, no matter how smart you are, you have plenty of weaknesses). Additionally, affiliate marketers do not work in isolation.

Most of them are friends with the marketers they sell products for; and this gives them far more leverage and information than you have access to. So start thinking of yourself as a business owner, rather than a completely self-sufficient Internet marketer.

Tip #2: Concentrate on Regular Sales

Regular sales are easier to quantify and predict; and, for this reason, it is far easier to continually ramp up small, regular sales until you are making hundreds of thousands or millions of dollars each year. So don't worry if you're the top affiliate for some major new product launch. Instead, focus on regular sales and regular increases in sales.

Tip #3: Do What They Do - Not What They Say

Observe the channels of marketer through which he promotes his product. Watch carefully to determine what methods he's using to make sales, so you can replicate his successes, rather than chasing after dreams he's written about.

Chapter III
How To Generate Passive Income In Affiliate Marketing

Today, affiliate marketing has become a very popular method of making money online. One can setup a passive income empire just by joining a good, rewarding affiliate program.

To be honest, you just can't expect to make decent money not doing anything. In affiliate marketing, the seller has already completed 50 percent of the task and you have to do the rest and make a profit.

You have to follow a good, proven method to promote your affiliate items and ensure high conversion rates.

Once you have reached the goal, you will be making a lot of money from that autopilot income stream.

How To Generate Passive Income In Affiliate Marketing

The Basic Steps You Must Follow:

Don't expect a sudden rise in your income few days after joining an affiliate program. You have to adopt a system that works; you have to follow a blueprint that can help you rank better on the search engines and generate visitors in an automated way.

Let's explore the basic steps you should follow while setting up your affiliate marketing passive-income Empire.

#1 Prepare A Website/Develop Your Platform

If you're willing to setup a powerful passive income generator, you have to prepare the platform accordingly. You have to develop a professional website to promote vendors products and earn commissions. A professional website will be able to generate more organic traffic from the leading search engines. You should think about hiring a professional developer or an agency to help you.

#2 SEO: On-page and Off-Page optimization

Now you have to promote your website and optimize the pages for the search engines. Only with quality content and proper marketing plans, you can rank #1 in the leading search engines quickly.

You should follow a proven tactic to outweigh the competition and grab maximum leads from the organic sources.

You should also be able to invest for promoting your websites on different networks. A combination of on-page, off-page SEO and paid marketing can help you attain top SERPs.

#3 Get Social Buzz From The Social Media Websites

Today, the search engines are giving more priority to social media websites and their signals towards other businesses online.

Social media marketing (SMM) was an integral part of off-page SEO even a few years back, but now, this has become a standalone strategy to market your product/service online.

You have to get a natural social buzz from the leading websites like Facebook, twitter, pinterest, Instagram, etc.

#4 Stay Connected And Update Your Website Accordingly

Once you have ranked in the first page in a leading search engine like Google, you'll receive a lot of traffic from the organic searches.

The visitors will convert better than other sources and you will earn decent commissions. But this won't run autopilot forever; you have to stay connected with your readers and update the information whenever necessary.

You should also try to supple your visitors with fresh, new, interesting contents.

Chapter IV

Earn Passive Income Online - Simply Set It Up, Relax And Earn Good Money

Over the years, we as experts in affiliate marketing have come to the discovery that a recurring passive income is the best when it comes to affiliate marketing. Before now, we use to think that making money with websites like Clickbank, JVzoo and

Amazon is the best way to make money online from the comfort of our home. But sooner than later, we learned that creating a recurring passive income stream from a reliable affiliate program is something we cannot overlook.

This section aims at showing you what recurring passive income is all about and possibly show you the best recurring affiliate program you could ever choose.

What is a recurring passive income?

Before I proceed, let me breakdown the two terms, the term recurring or passive income simply means happening over and over again.

When we say recurring, we could mean something that reoccurs over a course of time. In summary, a good example to drive home this point would be, "a NETFLIX subscription. Month after month, people pay to get access to this service."

And the term income, it simply means the revenue received from a certain amount of business transaction. When a company talks about revenue, it simply means the money or profit. So when we say recurring income, we can also say repeating profit.

Now, what do you need to make a recurring passive income?

There are several ways you could earn a recurring income, it can be offline or online, but in this aspect of the eBook we are going to be focusing on the online aspect. We are going to be learning how to make huge residual or recurring income online.

As stated earlier, there are several ways you could make recurring income through various affiliate programs. For example, you have probably heard of Amazon Affiliate program.

These affiliate programs allows individuals to make money from the customers they send to them. If you can send a customer to Amazon and the customer makes a purchase, you get paid a certain percentage.

However, you can still make money with these types of program, but the only downside is that you have to constantly work to get people to buy. Doing the same work over and over again, if you ask me, I would say this is not a recurring or passive income.

You have to regularly look for customers to buy through your affiliate link. I know you would not like this very much, especially if you are the lazy type.

How about doing the work ONCE and earning over and over again for that same work?

This is the key to residual passive income online!

So now what is the solution to making a passive affiliate income without regular work?

The answer is simply look for a program that charges users on a monthly basis to keep using the service. If you discover that it is something your friends would like, all you need is to refer them and as long as they keep using the product or service, you will always get paid.

I guess you are seeing the beauty of this now.

Your one time effort keeps bringing you passive income without lifting a finger further after they have joined. This is by far the best way to make a recurring income online.

However, there is a problem. We have discovered that so many recurring income affiliate programs come out with high hopes of making you good money for a very long time, only for you to discover that after some time, they pack up and go, and all your efforts aimed at earning a residual income has been shattered.

But never to worry, we have done the hard work for you. We have seen and been working with a very reliable company for a long time, and they are not going to end anytime soon.

How do you know if a recurring income affiliate program is worth joining?

There are several factors that could be looked at when joining any affiliate program, especially when you are looking for a long lasting recurring income.

The first thing to consider is how long has a company been offering the service or product you are going to be promoting?

For example, a hosting company like Godaddy has been in the business of providing hosting and domain name for a very long time. Now, their kind of affiliate program is something you can be proud to join.

Second, know their payment terms and methods. How do they pay? How much commission do they offer? When do they pay? Do they offer seamless payment methods? You should ask all these questions when looking to join any recurring income affiliate program.

You do not want to join a program only to discover that after generating sales, you find it difficult to get paid. Always watch out for this when joining any program.

Third, you have to seek for testimonials of honest users. What do other people say about the program? Did anyone have any success with it?

All these are just few basic questions you should look into before becoming a affiliate marketer.

Chapter V

10 Things You Didn't KnowAbout Affiliate Marketing

Most people have heard of affiliate marketing. Affiliate marketing is basically referring people to various products and services around the internet.

For each sale you generate through your affiliate link, you earn a commission. The size of the commission depends on the products themselves, who is selling them and the percentage offered by the seller to the affiliate.

But what is actually involved in affiliate marketing? What do affiliates do on a daily basis? How do they earn money and how do they learn what to do?

An Example Of A Successful Website

There are several ways of marketing products and services online. Many affiliates create a blog first and sell products and services through their blog.

Martin Lewis has a very successful website called moneysavingexpert.com.

This website makes money by sending website visitors to various offers. If a sale is made through this website, the commission is credited to this website owner.

By creating content, offering value and helping people make sensible choices, the website has built a reputation and become more prevalent over time.

Google ranks this site highly in the search engines and thousands of people use it to make purchasing decisions every day.

How Can I Get Started As An Affiliate?

Affiliate marketing is huge. There are thousands of people already making their main source of income from the internet.

To get started as an affiliate you need to learn some basic strategies and build various methods of generating traffic from the internet to those offers. A lot of affiliates start with a simple blog.

Many travelers 'blog' about their travels. If you don't have a passion or interest to blog about, you can start by following an online course which will help.

How Long Does It Take To Make A Living?

Some people go into affiliate marketing with the intention of creating a second income. Some people want to make big money.

Depending on how much time you can dedicate to your affiliate business, and how dedicated you are to it, is a big factor in determining your results. Results vary from person to person.

With a large advertising budget and the right business model, some affiliates have replaced their living in 6-12 months. For others it can take years before it replaces their existing income.

Depending on your approach, advertising budget, and business model, it can take between 3 months and several years to build it to a point where it can replace an existing income.

Can Anyone Do It?

One of the great things about affiliate marketing is that the technology is now available to allow anyone to build their own online business.

As long as you are prepared to learn and implement that knowledge, anyone who can operate an email, can use online platforms and tools to build their own online business.

The main thing you need is the desire to learn. Affiliate marketing isn't for everyone though. It does take a lot of hard work and it can take years before you are rewarded financially.

What Are The Pitfalls Of An Affiliate Business?

You need to dedicate some time to your affiliate business for it to work for the long term. Some people go into affiliate marketing thinking it is some magic pill which will pay them instantly in cash.

Much like a job you can't expect to get out more than you put in. Affiliate marketing is performance related.

This means you don't get paid unless you can successfully sell products and services online. If you don't know what you are doing it can take years to do this.

You can't be a dabbler and expect to earn the big money. The big earnings are created over years of hard work. Don't expect to achieve this with only a small amount of input.

What Are The Best Things About Affiliate Marketing?

Affiliate marketing offers an incredible amount of flexibility and freedom. You can work an affiliate business from anywhere in the world providing you have a laptop and an internet connection.

You can choose your own hours and build it up around existing work. Many people come into affiliate marketing because it offers this kind of flexibility.

They can choose their priorities in life, spend more time with family, choose your working hours, travel and work abroad. No more commuting to work or working long hours for a boss you don't like.

Affiliate marketing also offers incredible scalability. A business which is local is always limited to the people who can travel to that business.

An online business can be global. Using digital products in conjunction with a global reach, you can scale using tools and software to reach thousands of people through digital technology.

By using automation much of the work involved with an online business can be pre-built. By building automation into the business model, you can focus your activities on reaching a larger audience through content creation and paid advertising.

Why Am I Struggling With My Affiliate Business?

A lot of people struggle with their affiliate businesses.This can be for a number of reasons. First, building up an affiliate business takes time.

You need to dedicate a lot of time to an affiliate business in the first place. Only when you reach a 'tipping point' do you really start to see your progress.

Many affiliates simply don't realize how much work is involved. They underestimate how much time they need to dedicate to their online business to make it work.

Paid advertising allows you to grow your affiliate business quickly. But it costs money and you need the right products too.

You can't advertise small value items with paid advertising. You won't generate enough profit to cover your advertising costs.

You need a range of products and an email list to advertise through.

Content marketing takes much longer to work, depending on your chosen area of business. If you find an untapped niche to market your blog in, you can make some fast progress.

However, with a competitive niche you will struggle to get noticed above all the other content which you will have to compete with. There's several reasons why you might struggle.

The main one is lack of knowledge. Get the right education first and your affiliate business will move much faster.

What's The Best Affiliate Model To Use?

There are many different affiliate models all offering something different to suit the individual. Some affiliates target search traffic and aim to get their content found on Google. Some create their own products and sell them directly to customers.

However, having a range of products which you can sell over and over to existing customers is a great model for long term success. Selling a single item online is limited. It means you can only make one commission from each sale.

By choosing membership products to promote which also offer back end sales and a built in sales team, you can benefit from monthly commissions and up-sell commissions for the lifetime of any given customer.

Selling membership products is definitely a game changer when it come to affiliate marketing because you make an income from each customer, rather than a single commission.

But a good model to choose is one in which you have a passion for and can keep doing for the long term.

Choosing products which you have no interest in is a short sighted plan. Think about what you would like to do online to generate an income.

If you choose to go with your passion, your business will last much longer, and be more successful.

Can I Just Sell My Own Products?

Many affiliates create their own products to sell online. However, when you are starting out it is a good idea to learn the basics of marketing first. That way you can start earning more quickly from your affiliate business.

I spent a long time creating my own products when I first discovered affiliate marketing. But I didn't sell anything because of a couple of reasons.

First, I didn't research whether my products would have a big enough demand. Second, I didn't know how to market them.

By joining a program which teaches you how to market products first, you can start making money more quickly.

Don't waste time creating products if you don't know how to sell them. Marketing is a much more important skill for making money online.

Once you know this skill, you can then apply it later when marketing your own products and services. Also your own products will be limited in range.

By using an existing product range, you can benefit from products which are already selling. You can choose a program which offers high ticket commission, monthly memberships, back end sales and a built in sales team.

Building your own products which offers all of these things not a possibility for most people when starting out.

What's The Point Of Affiliate Marketing?

Some people struggle with the concept of affiliate marketing. They think it sounds too 'salesy'.

When I understood affiliate marketing I immediately found it appealing simply because I needed a flexible way to work around my contract work.

I had to drop what I was doing at a moments notice if the phone went. This meant other jobs were awkward to juggle around.

No- one wants to employ a 'flaky' employee. I wanted to work from my laptop and affiliate marketing gave me that opportunity.

For many people this is the reason why they choose affiliate marketing. They can earn an income from their laptop, choose their working hours and not have a boss or place of employment.

You don't have to sell directly to anyone or even talk to a customer. There is no stock to hold. Added to this, the scalability of affiliate marketing which lets you scale up to a global audience and deliver products on autopilot, makes it the best flexible business of the future.

Chapter VI
Affiliate Marketing Income: Step-by-Step Guide To Passive Income

By now you may have heard of internet bloggers, marketers and influencers talking about how much they earn through affiliate marketing income.

You've probably heard of stories of people who will tell you that their bank account had more money after they returned from vacation than they left a week prior.

Too good to be true? Not in the slightest!

Entrepreneurs have been earning affiliate commissions for years how and the best part is, it's never too late to jump on board and start earning with it.

Residual Income

If you're new to online marketing, affiliate marketing is one of the best ways to grow your income. In fact this is how most people start making residual income online.

Why? Because you don't have to go through the headache of any of the following: product research, surveying the market, merchandise, storage or product shipment.

Everything is done for you!

So, if you're intrigued to learn more about what affiliate marketing is, what goes into it, how you can profit big from it, and more details most people won't tell you about, read on!

Everything you need to know about affiliate marketing is right here within this guide, I recommend you read this book more than once so you can get better understanding of it.

Typically, there are four parties involved in the entire process.

1. The product creator
2. An Affiliate Network
3. The affiliate marketer
4. The end user (customer)

The Product Creator

Usually, this is a solopreneur or company that has an idea of a product. They create the product on their own or hire a team to develop it.

Often times the product will be in a digital format, however, developing products of all kinds is possible.

If I could throw a number on it, I would say about 90% of affiliate marketers start out using an affiliate network to find and promote products.

The Affiliate Network

An affiliate network acts as a "hub" between the product creator and the affiliate marketer. Product creators upload their products to a network and affiliate marketers come here to find their products and promote them.

Why would a product creator use an affiliate network instead of just deal directly with an affiliate marketer?

This is a great question. Although it's possible to completely leave an affiliate network out of the equation, there are some perks for a product creator to use them.

Affiliate networks usually have hundreds, if not thousands of products for affiliate marketers to promote.

Remember, 90% of affiliate marketers come to these networks to find a product to promote, so, with this in mind, if a product creator uses an affiliate network for their products, they have a higher chance of their products being found by affiliates to promote.

This can be very beneficial to product creators who don't have a huge list to push their products out to.

Clickbank and JVzoo are among some of the most popular affiliate networks.

Another company that has an affiliate program worth mentioning is Amazon.

Amazon has millions of products beings purchased on there website with billions in revenue and you can take your slice of the pie with their Amazon Associates program.

It's free to sign up as an affiliate and you can start promoting products immediately. Later, I'll show you an example of promoting Amazon products.

Chapter VII
Why Affiliate Marketing Is the Best Way to Start an Online Business

Now that we've discussed the different parties involved with affiliate marketing, let's talk about how to actually start making money.

As a Product Creator

Creating a product for affiliates to promote is a very leveraged way to make an income. So, how to create a product and start making money through affiliates?

The first thing you'll need to do in come up with a product idea. I don't recommend creating a product from the first thing that comes to your head. Instead, take a look in a niche and see what is in high demand and create your product based on what the market actually wants.

Another way to come up with a product idea is to survey your list (if you have one). Ask exactly what they need help with most. Using these two methods will get you on the right track to creating a profitable product.

Creating Your Product

Here are some valuable resources for creating your first digital product:

Next, you'll need to actually create the product. There are several different ways to do this, but I'll give you an example.

Since I've already shown you a network called Clickbank, we'll discuss how to create your product and put it on this affiliate network.

One option for creating products is through a site called *Optimizepress*.

This is site that allows you to create a website (WordPress theme), landing pages, sales funnels and membership portals. Any marketer who's been online for a good amount of time has heard of them.

Another option to create products that's increasing in popularity is *Clickfunnels*. While, Optimizepress does have everything you need to create a product, their sites are not as user friendly as Clickfunnels.

Clickfunnels specializes in high converting sales funnels. They also have landing pages and membership portals.

Another website of note for creating products is Teachable.

Teachable specializes in online course creation and is a fantastic place to start. Their interface is very easy to work with for both the product creator and course students.

Teachable allows course creators to bring on affiliates through their platform, so we won't be using them as an example for this.

After you create your course in either Optimizepress or Clickfunnels, you will need to integrate it with Clickbank.

Congratulations! Now that you have your product on clickbank, you can bring on affiliates to promote it and start making passive income.

Attracting Affiliates To Your Product

Now that you have your product, you want to bring on as many affiliates as possible.

If you have a blog, I recommend you start making blog posts that will attract more affiliates.

Also, use other social media platforms and your email list to notify people of your product and affiliate program.

As An Affiliate Marketer

Now for the fun part and why you're probably here to begin with. There are many ways to make money as an affiliate marketer. I'm going to show you a few right now.

Sign Up With An Affiliate Program
In order to make money as an affiliate marketer you must be signed up as an affiliate.

There are many networks to get started. Sign up with at least one so you can start promoting. For this example, let's say you're an affiliate with Amazon Associates.

Once you're a member of the affiliate program and logged in, when you search products on the main Amazon site, you'll have an added bar along the top that allows you to grab your affiliate link.

Creating Product Reviews

This is a long-tested, tried and true way to make money with affiliate marketing.

The process is simple. Find a product in your niche that you can make a good review about. Create a review and incorporate a call to action to purchase the product through your link.

Of course there are many different platforms you can create your reviews on, but the first one I recommend is through a blog.

Blogs can give a call to action to find the product on Amazon. The blog can have a link which is an affiliate link and when someone clicks through to Amazon and makes a purchase, cha-ching!

Another way to promote affiliate products is by making video reviews on YouTube.

Don't underestimate the power of YouTube. This is the second largest search engine in the world and get loads of traffic.

Sean Cannel has done a great job with affiliate marketing on his YouTube channel Think Media TV.

In his video published on December 15 2017, he gave a list of 7 different tech gift ideas on Amazon.

This is a creative way to do multiple reviews in one video and increase your potential for income.

Let's talk about the next way to make money as an affiliate marketer.

Product vs Product

Instead of creating a review about a single product or service, this method is creating a review of a product features and comparing them the features of another product.

This is a great way to drive traffic to affiliate links because people are always comparing products, looking to find which one is better.

It's also very highly targeting buyers in the marketplace. Usually, when someone is searching for "product vs product", they are in a position to buy and are looking to figure out what the best buy is.

This is where you can insert yourself to the equation by providing them with an in-depth comparison of both products.

Add your affiliate links and that's it!

Recommend Things You Already Use

If you've already started any form of online marketing, chances are you're already using tools and resources that have an affiliate program.

Simply share with people the tools and resources that you've used or recommend.

A great way to do this is through a "Tools, Resources or Recommended" page on your website. Put the a link to this page in the header of your website for easy access.

On this page, list out the tools and resources you recommend with affiliate links to all the products.

6-Figure Super Affiliate Strategy

I've shown you real ways to make money with affiliate marketing that you can literally start implementing today.

These strategies are proven to work. Hell, people are making six and even seven figures with what I've already shown you. But, now I'm going to share with you what will skyrocket your commissions. This is exactly what the millionaire affiliates are actually doing.

Let's get into the "juicy" stuff.

Build An Email List

No matter what niche you're in, one of the most important things you can do as a marketer is build an email list of subscribers.

If you plan on building a successful business online and you are not using both a capture page and an autoresponder, you are behind.

For those of you who don't have these, stop reading this post and go set them up. I've listed two of the best landing page and autoresponder services on the market here for you to get started with.

* (ClickFunnels) Landing Page/Sales funnels

* (Getresponse) Email Marketing/Autoresponder
Why is building an email list so damn important? One word my friend...

When you build an email list of subscribers in a specific niche, they are interested in what you have to offer, which can be the most leveraged thing you can have in your business.

Let's say for instance, that you are brand new to affiliate marketing and you want to promote a product. So, you find a something that you're happy to promote and believe your target audience will benefit from it and would be happy buy.

Let's also say that I pick same exact product to promote as well, only I've done the work of building an email list of thousands of people who I know are more likely to be interested in that product.

Who do you think will make more sales?

If you said the person with the bigger list, you're right. When you consistently have leads/subscribers coming into your email funnels, you'll never have to worry about running out of customers again. So, how do you go about adding people to your list? Great question!

How To Build An Email List

In order to build your list you will need two softwares. I've mentioned them already, but I'll give you one more chance to get them if you haven't already. If you've already have these softwares, then you're good.

Clickfunnels & Getresponse

Once you've setup your accounts you now have the tools to start building your email list. So what comes first?

Create A Lead Magnet

Creating a lead magnet is the first and most crucial step to start generating leads and growing your business.

There are many types of lead magnets you can create to start collecting emails: Cheat sheets, guides, reports, video courses, toolkits, ebooks etc.

Here are some things to keep in mind when creating your lead magnet:

It must be **FREE** - If you charge for your lead magnet, your conversions will dramatically decrease. Most of the time this is because people don't know who you are at first. So, they don't trust you enough to buy a product from you.

Trust me on this one, keep it **FREE**.

It must be **SIMPLE** - Although you may come up with 1,000 different ways to help people in your niche, the reality is they are not going to read your 10,000 page ebook or 25 hour free e-course. Make sure your lead magnet is simple, yet helpful.

It must be of **VALUE** - This is the most important part of your lead magnet.

Actually put time into thinking about what your ideal client needs help with and create your lead magnet to specifically help them with this problem.

Create something that you would actually charge money for, then give it away for free.

It must be **SPECIFIC** - Take the time to go deep into the mind of your ideal client. What's the one or two things they really need help with. Figure out what keeps them awake at night. What drives them? If you can create a lead magnet specifically to cater to this, your conversions will skyrocket.

How To Create Your Lead Magnet

There are many different ways to create your lead magnet, but I'm going to share with you two very simple ways to do this.

1. Canva.com

Canva is a creators dream. Their platform is simple and packs a punch. Once you create an account with Canva, you will have access to tons of online digital creation tools that you can use for free.

In this case, we want to navigate to the Ebook to create our free lead magnet. Once inside the Ebook section, type out your free lead magnet.

Keep in mind that you can link to other websites and tools within your lead magnet to further help your subscribers.

Income Tip: Use affiliate hyperlinks within your lead magnet to sources you recommend to increase your profits.

Once you have your lead magnet created, you can publish it right within Canva and get a unique URL for it, or download it and re-upload it elsewhere. You can upload it straight to your website, to dropbox or host it within Clickfunnels if you're using them as your landing page service.

2. Google Docs

So many people forget about Google resources, which is sad because it has so much to offer; one of which is their Google Docs.

Creating a document with Google Docs is very simple. Once you're logged in, simply create a new document and type out your new lead magnet.

Once you've finished creating your lead magnet document, you need to publish it to the internet with a specific URL. This url is what you'll be sending people to after they optin to your landing page.

You do this by clicking the share button at the top right of the document. After you click the share button, you will need to name your document. Give your document a name then hit save.

The next screen you'll see is how you'll be able to share it with others. You can directly send it to people via email or get a shareable link. In this case we want to click on Get shareable link at the top right.

The next screen is your final step in obtaining your shareable link.
You will see the URL you will copy and send people after they optin to your lead magnet. And that's it, you've created your lead magnet. Still reading? Bookmark this page so you can come back.

Create A Capture Page

Now that you've created your lead magnet, you need a way to present it online and capture leads. You'll do this with a lead
capture page.

A capture page has many names:

* Capture page
* Landing page
* Lead page
* Squeeze page
* Opt in page

So many different names, but it has one purpose. To collect emails.
There are many different platforms to create a capture page with, take your pick.

Once you've completed your capture page with your chosen software, you will integrate your email software with your landing page.

This is necessary to deliver your lead magnet via email, which brings us to the next point and a very important one at that.

Automate Your Business

Let's talk about how to leverage automation in your business. This allows you to leverage technology to grow your business in your sleep.

Passive income

Those stories you hear about people waking up to money in their bank account are true, and you can do the same thing in your business.

How does this work? With email automation

You will set this up with an email autoresponder. An autoresponder allows you to deliver your lead magnet automatically to your subscribers and follow-up with them through automation sequences.

Now, you can alter what emails you send to people based on their specific actions. So, if they didn't open the email for your lead magnet, you can send just those specific people a tailored email to remind them of the free gift you've have for them.

Setting up these tailored emails is called a workflow.

You can be even more specific and send emails based on whether or not someone has clicked a link inside a specific email. And remember, all this is automated. Very powerful.

The Secret Sauce To Go Full-Time

What are the 6 and even 7 figure earners doing to create such massive success, and how can you do the same in your business?

That's what I'm going to share with you right now! So pay close attention.

Build A Brand - Even If You're Brand New

No matter what niche you're in, you'll find that the top affiliates build a brand. But, what goes into building a brand and why would you want to do this?

Building a brand means people will trust you. They see you as an authority in your niche and as the "go-to" person for information on a given topic.

If you're just starting out and feel that you can't do this, keep reading, because I'm going to share with the secret to growing your brand, even if your brand new.

Step 1. - Identify Your Strengths

What are you good at right now? This is very important to figure out because you're going to leverage this to grow your brand faster.

Not doing this one thing is one of the most common mistakes people make in growing any online business. They focus on strengthening their weaknesses and start marketing based on their weaknesses. This is stupid. Let me explain...

If you had a successful business and were about to launch a big product and needed to find someone to be in a video commercial for your new product, how would you find them?

You would probably hire someone for the job who excels at being on camera, would you not?

An actor or an actress. Why?
Because they are good at what they do.

Now, let's take it back to growing your brand.

If you suck at being on camera, you don't want to start shooting YouTube videos as your primary method of growing your brand; like I said, that would be stupid.

In no way am I saying you shouldn't work on your weaknesses, you absolutely should, but if you're treating your brand like business, you don't want to use your weaknesses as your number one marketing method.
Harness your strengths!

Use your strengths to grow your brand!

If you are great in front of camera, by all means, film away, but if you're better at written communication, start a blog or find forums to contribute to.

When you identify your strengths and leverage them to grow your brand, you are setting yourself up for creating success much faster, unlike those who use their weaknesses as a source to build their brand.

Step 2. Inundate The Market With Value

This is the secret sauce to making a name for your brand as a nobody. Start pumping out as much helpful information into the marketplace as you possibly can, and trust me, you will get a response.

Don't use the excuse "I don't have value to give". Even if you're starting out brand new, simply go learn some helpful information and share that information with the marketplace with your own flare.

Don't think this works? It does. This is exactly how I've grown my business to where it is today and I've seen plenty of other people do the same thing.

Here's one thing you must remember when building your brand.

You are your brand. Even if the same exact information exists out on the internet, some people will find more value from it when it's being shared by you. So, don't deprive them of getting information from you. If you didn't know it yet, there's a huge audience waiting to hear your voice, all you have to do is speak.

What Affiliate Marketing is NOT

If you get an unsolicited email inviting you to join an affiliate network and it's asking for an upfront payment, then you definitely have to scrutinize them and find out whether or not they're scam or legit.

Go to the Better Business Bureau (BBB) and find out about the company, if you can't find any, then go to affiliate marketing forums and discussion boards.

They would know a lot about these scam sites as news spreads fast in social media and forums.

Another thing to look for is if these people are selling you unrelated products or something that you will never be able to use, like the $350 "Secrets to Affiliate Marketing Success" book or some other catchy titles; although a few are genuine but they don't charge you that high.

The truth is you can learn basic affiliate marketing from top ranking websites and blogs. In fact, they can teach you more useful information than all those specialized books and DVDs that other people are selling.

Becoming an affiliate is free when you sign up to affiliate marketing programs and the only thing that will really cost you money is web hosting, which is around $70 - $100 a year for your affiliate marketing blog.

Types of Affiliate Marketing

What's interesting about affiliate marketing is that you can earn commissions in more ways than most people think. Allow me to explain the 3 different types of affiliate marketing and how you can earn through them.

1. Unattached Affiliate Marketing
- This type of affiliate marketing will not require too much work from you, you don't even have to setup an affiliate marketing blog like those for Amazon Affiliate Programs.

This is more like a PPC marketing (pay- per-click) where you just show affiliate ads on sites that allow this kind of marketing and then get a commission for each click through that web users make on the ads.

2. Related Affiliate Marketing

This type of marketing is where you are required to have some level of involvement and this is where you create an affiliate marketing blog or website and always show affiliate links on almost all of your website/blog pages. You also earn a commission for each time a web user clicks through the affiliate links.

3. Involved Affiliate Marketing -

This kind of marketing may require you to actually use the products/services before you write a review about them and you should be able to write a more comprehensive and honest reviews.

You can choose from these 3 types of affiliate marketing methods, but most affiliate marketing programs uses the Type 2 affiliate marketing, which has some level of involvement and online presence from your end.

Putting the Cogs and Wheels Together

Now that you have an idea of what affiliate marketing is all about and what its common pitfalls are, you are ready to start your journey to financial freedom and a wealthy lifestyle!

Affiliate marketing is just like any other type of business and you'll have to plan a strategy months or even years ahead before you begin, so I will give you the basic strategy of how to become an affiliate marketer, signing up for affiliate programs, setting up your affiliate marketing blog and all the other important details about it.

Steps to become an affiliate marketer:

1. Decide what niche topic you want to use for your blog or website. It's better to write reviews or general information about products/services that you're passionate about, because you will write better articles for them compared to those that you don't like.

For instance, if you're mad about crochet or kids bicycles, then that is the niche you should pick for your blog.

Affiliate programs have a huge inventory of items for sale and they do include crochets and bicycles for a fact.

If you're more of the business-minded individual and you think you can write just about on anything, then by all means pick the niche that's most profitable among the lot.

2. Create your website and purchase a cheap but reliable web hosting. You don't need a web designer to build a website or a blog.

You can use WordPress, Weebly, Web.com, Blogger, eHost and others to do that. Using their user-friendly "click & drag" features you can create your blog/website in 5 - 10 minutes!

3. Learn basic SEO and use it on your blog or website. Search engine optimization or SEO is a very good marketing strategy to allow your website to be known throughout the entire internet or at least the majority of it. If your website is easier to find in search engines, then it is more convenient for people to visit it, and more visitors means more money for you.

4. Learn social media marketing to extend your presence online. In reality social media marketing or SMM is also a part of the grand scheme of SEO

and without it, your SEO campaign would not be as successful as you'd expect it to be.

There are literally billions of people hanging around the web on a daily basis and much of them are in social media sites. It would be a logical choice to get visitors there for your website and increase your income potential.

5. Learn about paid advertising and consider it deeply on whether you need to use it or not. Paid ads help because they target the right kind of people who are already looking for products that you promote.

Meaning there is a good chance that they will buy. Wouldn't you want them to buy products through your affiliate links? I would!

6. Start filling up your website with content. In case you plan to write boring and unimpressive blogs and

articles, then I'd advise you to no longer continue in your pursuit of creating an affiliate marketing blog, because I promise you people will not want to read your blogs or visit your site.

Write articles that will impress you first. This will let you know whether or not people will want to read about what you have to say. If you can find an extremely critical person to judge your writing, then that would be better as it will help you greatly improve on your writing style.

Reader engagement is absolute in affiliate marketing. It will determine your income capacity, so do your best in writing content for your site above all else.

How you earn in affiliate marketing:

• You'll need to embed or display affiliate links on your website or affiliate marketing blog about the products you're promoting. The purpose of these links is to guide your blog readers to the seller's webpage (which is usually in the affiliate network's site) so that they can make purchases of the items they like.

• The percentage commission on each sale range from 1% - 10% (some give more than 10% but rarely) and this is how you generate income.

For example, a web user happens by your blog about coffee machines and he/she read your blog review or informative article.

The reader was impressed by your blog and decided to click on the affiliate link, then make a purchase of 1 coffee machine worth $350. If the affiliate network allowed 7% of that amount to be your commission, therefore your income for that sale alone will be $24.50.

• You may notice that $24.50 is a small amount and not enough to convince you to become an affiliate; however, if you were able to bring 10,000 visitors to your blog in the span of 30 days and about 4,382 people bought coffee machines for themselves, then your income for that particular month should be $107,359!

If you're able to bring as much visitors to your website on a regular basis, then you can bet that your monthly income should be around these numbers.

Now you can appreciate the value that SEO and SMM can do for your affiliate marketing business.

How Much can you Make?

At this point I will let you use your imagination as to how much you can earn; or is it how hard you desire to earn.

It's entirely up to you. I am confident that this article should help you get started in creating your own affiliate marketing blog and earn not just money, but your freedom from the everyday worries of life.

Once you start earning over $8,000 a month, then you can buy more time to spend it with the people that matters to you most - your family.

Chapter VIII
Why People Fail in Affiliate Marketing Business

More and more people are lured into affiliate marketing and you might be one of them. Indeed, affiliate marketing is one of the most effective means of generating a full-time income through the Internet.

It's a fair deal between the merchandiser and his affiliates as both benefit from each sale materialized.

Like in other kinds of business, a great deal of the profits in affiliate marketing depends on the affiliates selling, advertising and promoting strategies.

Everyday, as affiliate marketing industry expands, competition heightens as well so an affiliate marketer must be creative enough to employ effective and unique ways to convince potential buyers to purchase available products and services offered.

Compared to traditional advertising practices, affiliate programs are more effective, risk-free and cost-efficient.

Reasons people fail in affiliate marketing

So why do many people still fail in affiliate marketing? There are a lot of reasons and a lot of areas in the program to look into.

The most critical aspect in the affiliate program is advertising. It is the most important factor in any kind of business as well. Many affiliate marketers fail in this aspect because they lack hard work.

Although it pays to be lucky, you cannot merely rely on it. Affiliate marketing isn't as simple as directing customers to the business site.

You must invest in yourself

If you want to earn big, of course, you have to invest time and great amount of hard work in promoting the products.

The competition is very high and customers nowadays are very wise, too, as earlier mentioned. After all, who doesn't want to get the best purchase? That is, to pay less and get more in terms of quality and quantity.

Being prepared is critical in affiliate marketing

Lack of preparation is also a reason why one fails in affiliate marketing, whether he is a merchandiser or an affiliate.

Part of the preparation is researching. On the part of the merchant, he has to be highly selective in choosing the right affiliate websites for his affiliate program.

In order to be sure he has the best choices, he must have exhausted his means in looking for highly interested affiliates whose sites are sure fit to his products and services.

The affiliate site's visitors must match his targeted customers. On the other hand, the affiliate marketer must likewise research on the good-paying merchandisers before he signs up for an affiliate program.

He must ensure that the merchant's products and services match his interests so he can give his full dedication and attention to the program.

He can get valuable information by joining affiliate forums, comparing different affiliate programs and reading articles on affiliate marketing where he can get tips from experienced affiliate marketers on how to choose the best merchants and products with high conversion rate.

Your website is critical to the success of your affiliate business

The website is a very important tool in the whole affiliate program. You should plan how your site is going to be, from domain name to the design, the lay-out, the content, and ads, as a marketer.

Some users are particular about what they see at first glance and thus when they find your site ugly, they won't spend their time looking at your site.

On the other hand, there are those who want information more than anything else. Marketers with "rich-content" web sites are usually the ones who prosper in this business because the content improves traffic to the site.

Websites with high quality contents and relevant keywords are the best optimized sites.

Having the right information about the product and service and not just a bunch of empty hyped-up advertisements will allow you to earn big in affiliate marketing even when you're asleep.

If you're not able to sustain the interest of your site visitor, you won't be able to lead them to purchase. No click-through means no sale and thus, no income on your part.

Selecting a top level domain name is also crucial to the success of the affiliate program. Lots of affiliate sites don't appear in the search engine results because they are deemed by affiliate managers as personal sites.

Major search directories and engines would think of your site as a transient one and thus, they won't list it in the directory.

Know first what you are going to promote before you decide on the domain name. Even if they feature the exact products the customer is looking for, the customer might think the site is not relevant and becomes weary of the site contents.

An educated affiliate is a successful affiliate

Above all, an affiliate marketer must be willing to learn more. Certainly, there are still a lot of things to learn so an affiliate marketer must continue to educate himself so he can improve his marketing strategies.

Many fail because they don't grow in the business and they are merely concerned about earning big commissions quickly.

If you want long-term and highly satisfactory results, take time to learn the ins and outs of the business.

Continue to improve your knowledge, especially with the basics in marketing ranging from advertising to programming, web page development, and search engine optimization techniques.

Likewise, study the needs and wants of your site users and how different merchandisers compete with each other.

If your initial attempts are failures, do not give up. Keep plugging away. Do not get disappointed.

You see, thousands are attracted by the possibility of generating skyrocketing incomes through affiliate marketing and so they sign up in any affiliate program without carefully understanding every aspect of the business.

When they don't get instant results, they quit and sign up for another program and repeat the process of just copying links and referring them to others. When you sign up for an affiliate program, don't expect to get rich in an instant.

Work on your advertising strategies and be patient. Stay focused and become the best student you can be and you will not be the one that crashes in affiliate marketing.

Chapter VIIII
Key Benefits of Affiliate Marketing

Since I decided to take the plunge few years ago and start working for myself as an online marketer, affiliate marketing has been the best thing I have ever been involved in and is now part of my daily schedule.

It is without a doubt something that all people who are interested in starting an online business should investigate and take up.

If you are undecided or have little knowledge about affiliate marketing then I hope that you find the below information helpful and that it will clear up any doubts that you have over what the key benefits of affiliate marketing are.

1. Commission basis

For the affiliate marketer this is a key advantage as every time that somebody makes a purchase, the affiliate receives a set commission of the profit.

For the affiliate merchant this is an advantage as they only pay the marketer when they make a sale, so no money is wasted on marketing spend.

2. Huge audience

For the affiliate marketer - having built up various marketing lists or websites, they can make use of their huge audience base and ensure that the traffic they send over to the merchant is qualified and that sales are made, making the affiliate more money.

For the affiliate merchant - they receive access to a wider audience base than they may have had before, creating more interest in their products, resulting in more sales and all without investing any more money or time.

3. Ease

For the affiliate marketer - once they have set up their additional sites and links across to the merchant, it is very simple to manage and often affiliates will continue to make money from sales without having done anything for months.

For the affiliate merchant - they do not have to invest time and money writing content or creating expensive images in order to promote their services/ products. Instead affiliates will apply to be a part of their programme and all the merchant need do is have many affiliates all working towards promoting their products/ services and wait for the sales to flood in.

4. Steady cost

For the affiliate marketer - building on the last point, an affiliate can keep receiving commission from sales of a product or service for years, despite not doing a lot of work to promote it. You do need to invest time at the start but then you have a regular source of income coming in for the market life of the service/ product.

For the affiliate merchant - they set up all the costs so the chance to make a huge profit on sales without having spent much on marketing, is very likely. They do not have to pay their affiliates much per sale to make the business relationship worthwhile, as it tends to work best on a quantity basis so everyone is happy with the set amounts.

5. Brand Visibility

For the affiliate - there is a lot to be gained reputation wise from working with a range of brands, and you will find that you get a lot more work should you be able to prove that you have succeeded with others in the past.

For the affiliate merchant - they receive free brand exposure on a continual basis, which is never a bad thing. If you have many affiliates working on promoting your brand, you'll soon see a boost in search engine rankings and online sales.

Amazon is an excellent example of where this has worked in the past.

6. Outsourced expertise

For the affiliate marketer - they get the continued experience to improve and work on their methods of online marketing, investing only their time not money.

For the affiliate merchant - they will be able to utilize all kinds of affiliates who are experts in SEM (search engine marketing) and SEO (search engine optimisation) without investing a lot of money, yet still manage to get to the top of Google rankings.

7. Transparency

For the affiliate marketer - through the various affiliate programmes, it is possible to see exactly when sales are made and payment is automatic, so you do not have to worry about chasing merchants for payments.

For the affiliate merchant - they can see and manage their R.O.I (return on investment) extremely easily and do not have to worry about tracking the origin of each sale.

8. Online market

For the affiliate marketer - there are an endless number of affiliate programs out there and the demand for online shopping is not going to decrease, so the earning potential for affiliates is huge.

You can access any number of markets with your affiliate work, whether you choose jewelery, health related, pet products, insurance or food.

Use long tail pro to find targeted long tail keywords with low competition, ensuring maximum affiliate sale for you.

9. Home-based work aimed at affiliate marketer

If you become successful in the world of affiliate marketing then it is entirely possible to create a long term Passive Income. added bonus is that you can work cheaply from home and you can be your own boss.

You don't have to pay to sign up to affiliate programs. They are all free to join.

10. Overcoming tradition (aimed at affiliate merchant)

Using affiliates to promote your products and services will guarantee that you receive a lot more exposure than you would by using more pricey traditional marketing methods.

Having a number of affiliates promoting what you are selling and only being paid when a sale is made, is one of the most cost effective marketing methods ever as well as being incredibly successful.

Chapter X
Affiliate Marketing VS Product Creation

This is a huge obstacle many people face when entering the online marketing world. Should I become an affiliate marketer or should I create and sell my own product..?

Before I get started, let me quickly define the two business models so that we are clear as to how money is generated with each.

• Affiliate Marketing: In this business model you will be making income by referring customers to another person's product or service. So basically you will sign up with the vendor as an affiliate and for every sale you generate you get paid a commission.

• Product Creation: This business model is pretty self explanatory; you will be creating a product and selling it in the marketplace for 100% of the profits. In this example we will be assuming your product is an information product of some sort.

There are a lot of marketers that will say the easiest way to start making money online is affiliate marketing.

Just because of the simple fact that you can choose a vendor whose product you want to promote, sign up as an affiliate, start sending traffic to your affiliate sales page and BOOM! You make money. Sounds pretty easy. You don't have to deal with creating a product, setting up websites, dealing with customers, etc.

At the same time there are marketers that say creating your own product is easier and the more profitable of the two and allow you to be more in control of your business.

It really all depends on what your strengths and weaknesses are and what you're looking to accomplish in your business.

Let me get some of the pros and cons of each and put things into perspective so you can have a better idea of where you want to get started.

Affiliate Marketing

It is a strong argument that affiliate marketing is the easier of the two to start with which is why it is recommended as a starting point for beginners.

Here are a few of the pros of affiliate marketing:

• Most affiliate vendors/networks are free and very easy to join. Most of the time you will answer a few basic questions, set up a username and password and get instant access to the affiliate member's area within a few minutes.

• Marketing materials are provided. Once you set up your profile in the affiliate member's area you will have complete access to all marketing materials needed to get you going such as banners, pre-written emails, etc.

In the members area you will also be provided a unique affiliate link which will take your prospects to a complete sales page which has already been created for you. Armed with these materials all you have to focus on is getting traffic to your affiliate site.

• All websites are already created for you. As an affiliate you do not have to deal with the headaches that can come with setting up a website. The vendor has done this for you and as long as you use your affiliate link your sales and commissions will be tracked through that link and paid into your account.

• Do not have to deal with customers. We all know how difficult it can be to deal with customers but as an affiliate you do not have to worry about this problem. Once you make a sale as an affiliate all you have to worry about is cashing your check and the customer is passed on to the vendor.

As you can see being an affiliate marketer definitely has its perks. It's quick and easy to join a vendor/network, all the marketing materials and sales pages are provided and you do not have to deal with customers. You can focus your time on generating traffic, making sales and cashing checks!

Now let's take a look at some of the cons of affiliate marketing and how you can overcome them.

• The competition. Even though it can argued that affiliate marketing is the easiest way to make money online it can be strongly argued that it's the most difficult due to the competition. There are hundreds of thousands of affiliate marketers you have to compete with to make a sale. At the same time many experienced marketers agree that most new affiliate marketers do not know what they're doing since it's such an easy business to get into.

- One of the best ways to overcome this obstacle is to educate yourself. Always be a step ahead of the competition by learning what the top affiliates are doing to give them that edge needed to make the sale.

• Profit Margins. As I mentioned before with affiliate marketing you are making a commission for referring a customer to a vendor as opposed to you being the creator of the product and earning 100% of the sale.

So there can be a lot of profits you are leaving on the table by promoting someone else's product instead of your own.

- This obstacle is really not in your control when it comes to affiliate marketing but the best thing you can do is promote a product with a higher payout of 60-80% as opposed to 25-50%. This way you will be making more income with less sales.

• Building someone else's business. As an affiliate not only are you generating sales and profits for the vendor you are also helping them build their business instead of your own.

Once you make a sale and are paid a commission that customer is now in the hands of the vendor which can continue to sell additional products and services to that customer for the lifetime of their relationship.

- The best way I know of building your own business through affiliate marketing while also sending customers to the vendor is to set up a landing page of your own that requires the prospect to input their name and email before they get access to the sales page. This way the prospect is on your customer list as well and you can now email them future offers and affiliate products directly.

Now of course you will have to provide an incentive to the prospect for them to enter their email like giving away a free report, video training, audio file, etc. We will touch on this in a future report.

• Lack of control. With affiliate marketing you really don't have much control of anything but generating sales. Should the vendor/network decide to shut down or no longer sell the product you are promoting you are left back at square one.

When it comes to product creation you have a lot more control of your business and can profits but we'll be touching on that in a few.

- Unfortunately this is a huge downside to affiliate marketing and something you really can't prepare for.

Building your email list as mentioned before is the best way to ensure that you still have an ability to make sales with your current list of customers while you set up a new campaign with a new product.

There are just as many cons as pros with affiliate marketing but none of these reasons should stop you from getting started if it's a business you wish to pursue.

One important thing that you want to keep in mind is to take time to invest in your education and skill sets to put yourself ahead of the curve. By doing this you set yourself apart from the competition and a step ahead to making the sale.

Now, just for a second picture yourself being the product creator and having an army of affiliates promoting your products as we move into the pros and cons of Creating and selling your own product.

Product Creation

Product creation can be a scary subject for many because as a newbie you are most likely skeptical and completely in the dark as to how an online business operates, let alone creating a product from scratch. But to your surprise, it can actually be one of the easiest ways to make money online.

Let's get into some of the pros of creating and selling your own product and see why it can be an avenue you consider:

• Control. When it comes to product creation you are in complete control of just about everything.

You are in control of how you market your product, the price, its delivery, and you are in full control of every customer you bring into your business as well as any future purchases they make from you.

• Profits. Of course this is a huge reason why many people create and sell their own products. As a product creator you get to keep 100% of the profits from every sale you make.

Now there is an exception to this when it comes to setting up your own affiliate program and having other affiliates promote your products but we'll touch on the power of this next.

• Affiliates. Once you create your unique product you can choose to leverage others to help build your business. Setting up an affiliate program can be a powerful way to explode your business on autopilot.

You can offer your affiliates a commission of 30-50% and have them sell their butts off for you, especially if your product brings high value to the marketplace.

Also you can make money while you sleep as you know your affiliates are working hard to make you sales.

• Building a Brand. Being the product creator gives you the opportunity to build a brand for yourself in the marketplace of your chosen topic.

Since your product is unique you are able to name the product whatever you like and build a brand around that topic.

This is very big if you want to build your business through word-of-mouth advertising which we all know is the strongest form of advertising.

As you can see there are also some great advantages to creating and selling your own product.

You are in full control of everything, you will earn more money, you can build an army of affiliates, and you can build a brand for yourself and your business. But as in everything there is a downside so let's get into that next.

Here are a few cons of product creation and how you can overcome them:

• Time. When it comes to your time, creating your own product will definitely take up more of your time then simply signing up as an affiliate.

Not only will it take time to create your product, but you also have to create a website to sell your product from. And that can be a headache of its own which we will talk about next.

The great thing about product creation is you can outsource just about every process involved in starting your business.

You can literally pay a professional writer to write your information product for you and you take the credit for it. Of course you always want to proof read it and modify a bit to fit your personality and style.

• Websites. Once your product is completed you will not be able to make any profit unless you are able to get it published online.

For some this can be your worst nightmare. This can cause you a lot of headaches especially if you are not tech savvy.

This can easily cause you to quit or never begin to try to make money online, or it can cause you to have to hire a web designer to build a site for you which can be a few hundred to a few thousand dollars in cost. This leads me to my next topic.

Again building a website can easily be outsourced to a web designer who can build you a clean professional website usually within 48-72 hours.

• Cost. When it comes to creating a product it can easily be said you will have more start up costs then an affiliate.

When it comes to setting up your sales funnel you have certain costs like buying a domain, hosting your website, hiring a web designer to set up you site unless you're doing it yourself, paying for the graphics to brand your product, etc.

A lot of you may be asking yourself how much are you going to expect to spend on your product creation business?

Don't worry take a deep breath..a lot of the things you will be paying for are really inexpensive.

You can buy a domain for about $10 and hosting is about $5 a month. Now I want to introduce you to a site that will dramatically change the way you do business it's called Fiverr.

This is a community of people that are willing to just about anything for $5. Go ahead and visit the site and see for yourself.

You can literally have an information product created on a topic of your choice, the graphics and ebook cover created, and a website build for $25-$30.

• Customer Support. As the product owner you will be responsible for your customer service and support and this alone can drive you insane and drain a lot of your time and energy.

As in any business, you will have your happy customers and your not so happy customers.

Your customers will have questions, demands, concerns, etc and it is your responsibility to make sure they get the support they deserve.

Customer support can also be outsourced, but unfortunately this comes with the territory of any business and something you will have to deal with.

Yes, you can have someone take care of your customers service but you should definitely be as involved as possible to make sure they are getting the best support possible.

As you can see as a product owner, yes you will be in control, yes you will make more money, and yes you can build a brand, but with all this comes a lot more responsibility then an affiliate marketer.

Before wrapping things up lets touch on a few things that we can all agree on in both affiliate marketing and product creation.

• Work from home. Whether you are an affiliate marketer or promoting your own products both allow you to be in control of your time and work from home.

For many this a highly sought after luxury to be able to spend more time with family, friends, spouse, etc.

• Your day job. Unless you are a super marketer and were born with super online business skills most of you will still be working your day job as you build your online business.

With that said you can build your online business on a part-time or full-time basis around your current work schedule whether it is one hour a day or ten hours a day, whatever it is that works for you make sure you keep it consistent. Make sure you schedule your online business time just as you would schedule any other activity and make this non-negotiable.

• You're the boss. No matter if you're marketing as an affiliate or your own product, you are your own boss in both situations and your income is directly influenced by your efforts.

This also allows you to make money on demand. If you're looking to take a vacation or buy a new car and you need a few thousand dollars you can just jump on your computer and set up a new marketing campaign.

There really is no right or wrong, better or worse, that was not the point of this article.

The point of this report was to shed some light on both business models so that you can be more aware of what you can expect in moving forward with your online business.

In my opinion there shouldn't have to be a choice between affiliate marketing and creating your own product.

You should integrate both into your business plan and become educated in both arenas.

By doing that you will quickly see that many top affiliate marketers make a killing selling their own products and many people who sell their own products make a killing as affiliate marketers.

One thing I do want to stress is no matter what you do it is going to take time, effort and hard work.

Don't fall into the trap that many newbie's do which is consistently searching for the next plug and play system that is going to make you the next overnight millionaire.

And there are plenty of "Guru's" out there who prey on the newbie community and put out junk products promising overnight millions with pretty sales pages and you continue to fall for them. STOP!!

Map out a business plan, decide what you want to accomplish, find one reputable mentor you want to follow and get to work!

Focus on following that chosen mentor all the way through to your first online dollar. And finally, make a promise to yourself that you will not quit before starting the journey!

Chapter XI

5 Winning Attitudes for Super Affiliate Marketing Entrepreneur

Have you ever thought of why you've failed whereas other affiliate marketing entrepreneurs are successful in promoting the same markets and affiliate products you do?

Within this article, you will discover and learn how to improve yourself as a super affiliate marketing entrepreneurs and learn top inside personal attitude of super affiliate marketing entrepreneurs.

1. Self-Determination

The first personality attitude is the determination. You have to push yourself moving forward toward to your goals. As an affiliate, you have to set up your goals, plan your works and push yourself toward to those goals.

Without this personality attitude, it appears that you will not move forward or closer to your goals and succeed in affiliate marketing business.

However, to setup your goals, you have to set them up as smart, measurement, achievable, and realistic goals.

The secret to affiliate millionaires is to push yourself to work out as your plan. You have to keep yourself stay in the path toward to your goals all the time.

2. Positive Thinking

Many studies reveal that there are two groups of affiliate marketing entrepreneurs: (1) people who can do anything and (2) people who can not do anything.

Those studies also reveal that all successful affiliate marketing entrepreneurs are in the first group, people who can do anything. It appears obvious that you are what you think you are. If you believe in yourself that you can succeed in the affiliate marketing business, you will definitely succeed in this business.

The secret to affiliate marketing is to change your negative thinking into positive. You have to change the way you think in the business. Of course, everything has two sides: good and bad. It is absolutely a great idea to underestimate the obstacles and try to find out the solution rather than giving up.

3. Self-Motivation

There are many obstacles to becoming a super affiliate. The real key to pass those obstacles is your self-motivation. You have to motivate yourself to move forward and solve all possible problems in your affiliate marketing business. You have to build, run and grow your affiliate marketing business everyday. You must enjoy what you are doing and you must motivate yourself enthusiastically at all the times.

4. Patient

The affiliate marketing business is not a get-rich-quick scheme. It will not come to you overnight or several weeks.

You have to be patient with your goals, plan and strategies you implement for your affiliate marketing business. Without the patient or faith, you will give up too quickly in this business.

Many studies reveal that all successful super affiliate marketing entrepreneurs are willing to work extremely hard and expect the results in the long-term.

5. Consistency

The last personality attitude for becoming a super affiliate marketing entrepreneur is to be consistent. By being consistent, it will definitely lead you to success in any kinds of business. You have to work out your plan year after year, month after month in order to ensure that you reach your goals.

The major different point between successful affiliate marketing entrepreneurs and failed entrepreneurs could be the personality attitude.
It can generate a huge difference in the long-term affiliate online business.

All you have to improve are:

- self-determination
- positive thinking
- self-motivation
- eager to learn
- Patient
- consistency

Chapter XII
Secrets to Affiliate Millionaires - 8 Steps to Run Multiple Streams of Affiliate Marketing Income

Obviously, running multiple streams of affiliate marketing income is a great idea to grow your affiliate commissions. You will maximize your profits online with multiple affiliate marketing strategies. You will discover and learn the basic steps to run multiple streams of affiliate marketing income.

You will leverage those simple steps and learn how to maximize your affiliate commission.

Affiliate Marketing Income #1:

Discover High Performance Keywords.

The first step is to discover high performance keywords for your affiliate marketing business.

With those high performance keywords, you will ensure that you can maximize your profits and earn huge affiliate commission.

To discover the high performance keywords, you can use pay per click (PPC) search engine to test and find out which keywords are super profitable for your business.

Without testing systematically, it is difficult to identify which keywords are profitable.

Affiliate Marketing Income #2:

Write Quality Relevancy Content with High Performance Keywords.

The next step for running success multiple streams of affiliate marketing income is to write quality relevancy content with those high performance keywords.

You have to build your own original content related to your niche market based on those high performance keywords.

Affiliate Marketing Income #3:

Build Your Website Ranking Based on Your Content.

The next step is to upload your content given from previous step on your website. You have to optimize your web page with those high performance keywords.

Also, there are many search engine optimization techniques on the internet to help you to build your website ranking in search engines.

Affiliate Marketing Income #4:

Consolidate Your Content into Your Own Article.

The article marketing is one of the most effective affiliate marketing strategies to drive quality relevancy traffic to your affiliate website.

All you have to do is to consolidate your content into articles. You have to focus on writing, article layout, article structure and article formats.

Additionally, submitting your articles to other article directories is a good idea to build up your reputation and creditability.

Also, it will help you drive more quality traffic to your affiliate website.

Affiliate Marketing Income #5:

Post Your Articles into Your Blog.

To run the multiple streams of affiliate marketing income, building your own blog with those same articles from previous step is a great idea.

However, you have to customize those articles for your own blog. There is a different point between post messages in the blog and article.

You have to put more of your personality and be more personalized into your blog. For blogging online, you have to build relationship with your readers.

Affiliate Marketing Income #6:

Include Your Articles into Your Newsletter.

Providing newsletter strategies has proven that it is very powerful to drive more traffic to your affiliate website.

Affiliate Marketing Income #7:

Participant in Forum through Your Articles.

Many studies reveal that participating in forums through your articles will help you boost affiliate commission and grow your affiliate marketing business.

The highest recommendation is to use this strategy properly, rather than trying to sell your affiliate products in the community.

You have to share and exchange the ideas and information related to your affiliate products among other people in the forums. That is the best way to maximize the power of forums and articles together.

Affiliate Marketing Income #8:

Place Online Classified Ads.

The last step to run multiple streams of affiliate marketing income with multiple affiliate marketing strategies is to place online classified ads.

With the content and highperformance keywords from above steps, you can conduct your own online classified ads.

The best approach to maximize profits from classified ads is to include proper keywords and benefits into your ads.

Conclusion

By now you should have learned how to combine several affiliate marketing strategies like pay per click, search engine optimization, article marketing, blogging and email marketing. The real key to your success for multiple streams of income is your creativity. You have to combine those affiliate marketing strategies together to maximize your profits.